Swimming with Turtles

Travel Narratives
Spirit of Place

Other Books by Doug Beardsley

Poetry

Going Down Into History
The Only Country in the World Called Canada
Six Saanich Poems
Play on the Water: the Paul Klee Poems
Premonitions & Gifts (with Theresa Kishkan)
Poems (with Charles Lillard)
Pacific Sands
Kissing the Body of My Lord: The Marie Poems
A Dancing Star
Free to Talk
Inside Passage
Wrestling with Angels
Rain Music

Non-Fiction

Country on Ice
No One Else is Lawrence! (with Al Purdy)
The Man Who Outlived Himself (with Al Purdy)

Anthologies

The Rocket, The Flower, The Hammer and Me
Our Game

Swimming with Turtles

Travel Narratives
Spirit of Place

Doug Beardsley

thistledown press

© Doug Beardsley, 2014
All rights reserved

No part of this publication may be reproduced or transmitted in any form or by any means, graphic, electronic or mechanical, including photocopying, recording, or any information storage and retrieval system, without permission in writing from the publisher or a licence from The Canadian Copyright Licensing Agency (Access Copyright). For an Access Copyright licence, visit www.accesscopyright.ca or call toll free to 1-800-893-5777.

Thistledown Press Ltd.
410 2nd Avenue North
Saskatoon, Saskatchewan, S7K 2C3
www.thistledownpress.com

Library and Archives Canada Cataloguing in Publication

Beardsley, Doug, 1941-, author
Swimmimg with turtles : spirit of place / Doug Beardsley.

Poems.
ISBN 978-1-927068-87-8 (pbk.)

I. Title.

PS8553.E13S95 2014   C811'.54   C2014-900745-0

Cover: Bead artwork of the Huichol Indian people **with thanks to Joe Diaz of the Tierra Huichol Gallery in Vallarta, Mexico**
Cover and book design by Jackie Forrie
Printed and bound in Canada

  Canada Council   Conseil des Arts   Canadian   Patrimoine
for the Arts   du Canada   Heritage   canadien

Thistledown Press gratefully acknowledges the financial assistance of the Canada Council for the Arts, the Saskatchewan Arts Board, and the Government of Canada through the Canada Book Fund for its publishing program.

*For Linnie, love of my life
who sailed these Mexican, Caribbean and Pacific waters
as my sensual, seafaring wife*

*& with particular thanks to Stephanie McKenzie
former student, now poet, professor, literary critic
& supreme editor in her own rite*

*& finally to a man I've never met
my imaginative, electronic editorial wizard, Michael Kenyon
whom I can only thank & echo
It has been a true pleasure working with you*

CONTENTS

MOURNING IN MEXICO

12 Layers That Last

13 In Cabo San Lucas

14 Buried Violence

15 The Beach Vendor

16 The Bats

17 Guadalupe Cathedral, Vallarta

18 St. Sebastien del Oeste

19 Dark Hummingbird's Dance

21 Zihuatanejo

22 Gold Medal Game

24 Tapachula, Izapa, Chiapas

CARIBBEAN ODYSSEY

26 There Are No Prizes

27 Stone Crab

29 San Juan

30 St. Thomas

31 St. Thomas Iguanas

32 Cutting Through Slaughter

34 Barbados

35 The Pearl Fishers

37 St. Kitts

38 Tortola

39 Half Moon Cay

40 San Juan II

41 San Juan Rite

REFLECTIVE RIVER OF STARS & STONE

44 Maria Antigua Guatemala

45 Dying of Thirst

46 The Maya Codex

47 Nicaragua Soldata

48 Swimming with Turtles

49 A Taste of Costa Rica

50 Sonnet on the Real Presence in Panama

51 Guayaquil

52 Somewhere Around Trujillo

54 Cuzco

56 Postcards from Cuzco

58 *That Moment Falling Through Air*

59 Latin American Poetics

SOUTH OF THE EQUATOR

62 Linnie

63 First Landfall at Nuku Hiva

64 Tahiti

65 The Power of the Marketplace

66 *The Vision After the Sermon*

67 Moorea

69 Bora Bora

70 Fiji

72 Samoa, September 29, 2009

73 Squire Stevenson Arrives in Apia

74 From the Journal of Stevenson's Wife

75 RLS

76	Flim Flam Island
78	*Terra Australis Incognita*
79	Macho Madness
80	Pamagirri Dances
81	Arkana (Auckland)

HULA HYMNS

84	First Sighting
86	Melville's Mountains
87	Messenger
88	Sacrificial Presence
95	Afterword

Every continent has its own spirit of place. Every people is polarized in some particular locality, which is home . . . The spirit of place is a great reality . . . Men are free when they are obeying some deep, inward voice of religious belief.

— D.H. Lawrence, "The Spirit of Place" in *Studies in Classic American Literature*, 1928.

. . . if you just close your eyes . . . Having got it, you will at once get all the rest; the key is there . . . for you to turn . . . Nothing is strange to you at such a moment . . . for underneath the purely superficial aspects of apparent change the old tide-lines remain. The great thing is to travel with the eyes of the spirit wide open . . . with real inward attention . . . If you get as still as a needle you'll get there.

— Lawrence Durrell, "Landscape and Character" in *Spirit of Place: Letters and Essays on Travel*, 1960.

Mourning in Mexico

Layers That Last

In the morning we don't know where we are.
Wood-latticed windows and balcony door
open to bird-of-paradise and palm
a possibility of the Far East?
But it's only Old Town, San Diego
fiesta village, the best of both worlds —
Yankee know-how and Mexican myth.

In Cabo San Lucas

Everything is two-for-one and no one.
And many come for action after dark
slammed together by massive waves of
margaritas: mammals with mottled skin
roosterfish, human tuna, humpback whales
all out-of-water flapping their last breath
at the Nowhere Bar, where owner Pablo
spins on his black barstool to overhear
confessions of those who drink to confess
rather than forget their former lives. And
everything is two-for-one and no one.

Buried Violence

The country that dreams itself in the light
murdered its dreamers in the marketplace
pried their mouths open till they revealed
their innermost beings, the *zocalo*
filled with chants & songs & shrieks
as those who dared to dream
died in eighteen Aztec ways.

This was one way they killed the future.

But it didn't work — Motecuhzoma
bedeviled by ancient prophecies of
returning gods recovering their rightful
inheritance, emerging from the haze &
mist on horseback, on mythological beasts
that drove the people to sleep for centuries —
the shadow side of man devouring corn tortillas.

The Beach Vendor

Augusto by name, *amigo* eternal, appears from
the sea, wrapped in blankets (it's winter here)
five hats atop his bronzed head, his back to the
Pacific & all the glories that have brought
mobs of *gringos* to this carefree Paradise.

If you so much as move an inch to escape the sun
or raise an eyebrow in amazement at something
you've just read he'll unfurl one arm like a matador
& his array of blankets becomes a kaleidoscope cape
that any damned bull would give his life for.

At *siesta* he permits himself to sit beside
a coconut palm, his blankets the divine fabric
thrown down by the gods. This is paradise &
what we come for he's known from birth, the sea he turns
his back on, the sand he wades through to sell his goods —
two hundred pesos for a *sombero* or baseball cap
(he'll take off half of that & come out ahead).

The Bats

Like burnt parchment blown by wind
ash swirling above chimney tops
paper airplanes launched in a playground
they leave their terracotta haciendas
at 7:20 each evening
the last rays of sun glinting
off their 92.5 per cent silver
wristwatches as they wheel
opening, closing, darting, dancing, dipping
whooshing with the wind in silence
black specks in ritual formation
until the absence of light
in their shadow world is
forever altered by the flower-scented night

Guadalupe Cathedral, Vallarta

Eight angels light Our Lady's Crown
two dozen gems of her ring, five palms
the mysteries of the Marian rosary.
All this world of glass lit by a Cross.
Evening shadows made by

municipal buildings block out
the church, conceal the army in full
battle gear, AK-47s swinging from
teenage hips like warning fingers.
The soldiers show force but no strength.

The priest clears his throat, swallowing fear.
He knows history is not on his side
his pendulant Cross a microphone
giving voice to four hundred *familia*
safe in their faith. These people remain

sure the soldiers won't slaughter their
babies kissing beneath the pulpit.
But the true believer is never far from
doubt in this country of death, the Mexican
face in a continual state of mourning.

St. Sebastien del Oeste

17th-century cobblestone donkey streets
red roofs, whitewashed adobe dwellings
held up by *chiplode* sent from America
to keep the empty family home pristine.

A town down on its luck, silver mines
shut, 600 where once 30,000 lived
two nights, two days from Vallarta by horse.
Silver shapes a man's soul.

In the Sierra Madre miners once refused
to work on Mondays, hung over from tequila
weekends with dancing girls in the cantinas.
In Mexico the solution to every problem is to shoot

the accordion-player — or the priest.
Rafael tells us the longer the roasting the
darker the bean, the darker the bean the less caffeine.
You go tell Rafael Mexico is running

out of musicians, farmers & priests.
Red soil, corn plantations, rows of agave
in the hills. On the way down our tour guide
strums his bottled water like a blue guitar.

Dark Hummingbird's Dance

No roads lead to Las Caletas
(another two days, two nights by horse)
while our seagoing pyramid cuts the waves
like a pelican diving into the sea
searching for something to feed on.

Hundreds of torches light up the shore
votive candles mark the way up
the steep serpentine path to the Aztec
theatre carved out of tropical palms.

Temple steps ascend to the starlit sky
where moon and Milky Way offer
whatever light they're able. Men's heads
spin, mad with terror. A native
flute plays above a snake-drum beat.

We fall to our knees & eat dirt
like phantoms in a shaman's trance.
Out of jungle air Dark Hummingbird drops
his helmet head, purple-plumed feathers exploding.

A cutting wind snuffs out whatever
flames he missed with his thunderous feet
a love story that dances on too long
attempts to take us through eternal night
till the sun rises & the pyramid steps

flame amazement & Dark Hummingbird dances
his bitter retreat until the sun sets
& he takes centre stage
for another haunting performance.

Zihuatanejo

For 2,000 years local fishermen
have hauled their boats onto the sands
at Paseo del Pescador, beneath
palms and the Sierra Madre del Sur.

At first light the deserted beach transforms
into a marketplace of portable
blue freezers and grey tarps overflowing
with roosterfish, jacks, snook and grouper.

Gringos scurry by to avoid the stench.
Men sporting long-peaked baseball caps and white
undershirts stand staring at last night's catch.
They are the bull sharks, the sea is their world.

These days they catch money instead of men.
They have taken the name of fishermen
but no longer know how to cast their nets
for the only catch that truly matters.

Gold Medal Game

I was a player.

In 1529 a rubber ball streaked across the sky like a comet.
Hernan Cortes, flashy offensive
forward of the Spanish Conquistadors

led his *donjuanistas* onto the water-filled field in a cosmic contest
against Motecuhzoma, dark defensive
angel-king of the Aztec Barbarians.

They met in Mexico City, both teams playing their hearts out
for glory, God, & gold — in whatever order.
The life of every player was on the line.

I fought beside eagle & deer against
hopping rabbit & cigar-smoking insect.
The last time I saw the scoreboard
it was 6-to-something.

We were burdened by our beaded capes, caps, head —
bands, ear plugs, lotus blossoms, nose bones &
back feathers, turbans, ornamental shells.

The game a bloody rite of passage:
each night the sun descended, was sacrificed
and arose the next morning. Toward the
end we lost heart & sometimes our heads.

Sweet rolls, cactus juice, corncakes and flower
fountains offered up to dwarfs & dignitaries alike
at the halftime fiesta. Every one of us who took part in this

prophetic game refereed by gods but played
by men knew it was history in the making
a game without end, a story for all ages.

A few centuries are all that remain
on the clock. Everything is still
up in the air, everything is still
undecided.

But I have dreamed this game
will one day end in our favour
a gateway will open. From the battlefield
I have seen its gaping maw.

When, at times, I feel no more
than a pawn, mere cannon-fodder, I
shake my body back, my very being awake
to shape, to remind myself

I was a player.

Tapachula, Izapa, Chiapas

We are on the road to ruin, cutting through
a lowland canopy of thick jungle
the meeting place of Mayan and Olmec.
Roosters in the rainforest, tangerine trees.
In a clearing we are set upon by
50-ton helmeted, colossal heads
with block faces, fat lips and flat noses
kings masquerading as players
the game the ancient Olmecs played with
rubber balls, stone hoops like hollowed stars.
We are told it doesn't matter who wins
the Rain God will decide which team will live
& who will die. Our tour group gathers on the
stone seats for resting between sets. Like
a colony of red ants, we scurry
away into a cacao orchard
seeking more than we can experience.

Caribbean Odyssey

Open up the window, let that bad air out.
— Buddy Bolden

There Are No Prizes
for Buddy, Duke, Michael & Stefan

Touch everything he might have got his hands on touching
twenty of his favourite things — boas, beads, beignets
belly buttons, beer bottles, feather hats, party hats
ceramic masks, hand-made masks, voodoo dolls, go-cups, mint
juleps, mango daiquiris, hitching posts, cast-iron grills
wrought iron railings and the sweet & lovely café au lait

along the route up Canal to Marais all the way
down Iberville in those days like the Mississippi
snaking down the disordered streets 'made marble by jazz'
Freddie and Bunk and Kid Allen's dad all mortal men
just trying to make music till a cat cries out from
the sidewalk: 'better stop trying and start playing some'

& Buddy leaps out of the second line falling to the
street out of his mind playing fragments half-finished phrases
playing that voodoo music & St Louis Cathedral hymns
at the same time a whole lifeline of unfinished stories
following him home to his grave washed up cornet
and clothes sinking into the blue Mississippi mud

his music a shucked oyster shimmying down from forehead
to foot the nude dancer beginning over again
with an instep flip the pure sheen of her shaven skin
shining in a St Elmo's fire of phosphorescent
sex, voodoo drums & Christian hymns no one could touch him
in this world whatever we turn to touch drives us mad.

~ 26 ~

Stone Crab

for Joe's

The deeper he goes
the better off
he is. When he can't
escape he graciously gives up

a chelae or two —
a claw is broken off
by human hands it breaks
at the proper place

& he burrows deep
in his sandy darkness
close to crustaceans, carrion
oysters and seaweed

protected from cobia, conch
grouper, sea turtle, all
living things that have appetites
he can never assuage.

In his dream deep down
patiently he waits, he
heals himself whole
once more twice-limbed.

He knows nothing of pagan plants
Christian crosses, mustard
sauce or restaurants, their secret
prayer of preparation

where his own worst enemies
sing his praises, cry out
'O *taste and see* this succulent delicacy
from the chilled-chelae sea'

for he has found a way to live forever.

San Juan

Who would have thought returning to
San Juan would feel like returning home
the asymmetrical cathedral spires
a light limestone beacon to reluctant travelers
duty-bound to the great white north, like you, my lady
lighting up first dawn, your un-tanned parts like top and bottom
beacons of a lantern guiding me to safety
& old San Juan: breakfast on the fourth floor terrace
of the Milano, down Fortaleza up
del Christi to the cathedral & tapa bar
courtyard of the Dominican El Convento
those mouth-watering marinated anchovies
& crab cakes a la Barrachina reminding me
of you again, my white & tan fantasy
 my egret, my eternal illumination.

St. Thomas

Broken cloud. Darkened doubt.
Everyone looks like Sonny Rollins
without ambition. Even the women.
Left-side driving a colonial hangover.
Alleyways lined with finely-art jewelry.
Royal Dane. Drakes Alley. Palm Passage.
Shoppingashore a legacy of the past.
Pirates Paradise full of skeptics.

Return after Compline with the Patron Saint.
Cut locks from shop-shutters. If anyone awakes
speak to them in the European language. Read
them their rights. Grab the gold. Cut and run.
To cut a long story short. Cut them down to size.
Cut them to pieces. Cut them into archipelagoes.

St. Thomas Iguanas

Drawn back from the beginning & without doubt
saints-in-waiting, they emerge
from their Procrustean caves, begin
spiritual exercises at first light
the rocks warming to a hundred

or more cold-blooded seminarians sunning themselves

till banana break when they surround
a dark High-Priest who bows
from the waist but no farther for fear of
their reptilian teeth. Blessed fifty times over
these prickly-spined creatures take their food on faith.

Cutting Through Slaughter

With smoke by day & fire by night
like a wax candle rising & falling
we cross the Caribbean, a two-day diagonal
slash southwest to Aruba at nine knots
450 nautical miles of undiscovered
sea till, on Christmas Day
515 years ago at this morning's moment
Columbus lost the Santa Ana, an anniversary
blessing for this Transatlantic Eden.
We sit at table and talk about that time

& wish we'd been the first sailor to lift his eyes
from the ship's railing & see the horizon
not as a horizontal line but as
Circe circled, encircling a world beyond
three continents and one ocean, a world
not a sphere but a pear, ships rising toward heaven
before time, a garden overflowing with water
falls, palms, luscious fruits, docile animals
who felt no need to hunt, & innocent
children, lambs waiting to be led.

At dinner we're armed with enough cutlery
to arm a small army. So far it's all 'smiles and
serviettes' with Gilberto, Juan McHenry &
sweet Becca & *familia* but the tidal
shift and a good Gewurztraminer can turn
all this cutlery into cutlasses (one more glass
and I'll do everybody in). It's all in the
swagger, the numbed fear, an attitude that's as easy
to pick up as a knife or fork in the main dining room
or on deck, wave upon wave bathed in blood.

Barbados

I can't see a green sugar-cane field, or a yellow
catamaran full of mahogany tourists
floating offshore without thinking of slavery,
the winch-chain a shivering echo of
twenty-four million shipped from Africa
after the Arawak and Carib had been killed off
or worked to death. Now, all the boys who work the beach
look like Miles Davis, and we whites continue to pay
for our crimes, the price of the past, a three-hundred-
and-fifty-year scar singeing our souls.
You want to lie on the sand? Five dollar.
You seek some shade? Five dollar. Shift your chair
into the sun? Five dollar. And we pay.

The Pearl Fishers

a found poem for Phyllis, who would understand

See how the bald men are invisible
in Bizet's inane opera, the scene
Ceylon, the period 'barbaric', the
execution a funeral pyre, the love

triangle strangled by a pearl necklace
from the deep, a veiled priestess
to protect them from the perfect sphere
that fills men with greed & drives them mad.

See how the bald men clad in loincloths
dive from the smacks manned by Spaniards
in the engravings of Margarita
the tall masts of the sailing ships etched

on the horizon, the full oyster nets
taken from sea to boat to land, as blacks
journey from free men to serfs to slaves, *gulls
floating over boats floating in the bay.*

In the water *from dawn to dusk, at depths
of four to five fathoms,* Bartholme
de las Casas sees the bald men as boys
seldom permitted to surface for air

tearing at the oysters till their hands bleed
the water swimming with sharks, the young boys
up for seconds till they're punched back down.
The cold water chills their marrow, the boys

choking on their own blood as pressure on
their lungs makes them hemorrhage from the mouth
while others are carried off by dysentery from
the extreme cold, their black hair singed, their

young backs one great salt sore. They have turned
into sea wolves, sea-monsters, some other species.
At Annadale Falls near Lake Grand Etang
we watch the young boys solicit money

from jaded tourists, then climb the steep cliff
rocks jutting into the abyss, something
still in their blood, their young limbs skilled
at emerging from their cold ancestral Hell.

Their bright teeth like white pearls
they play *in a watery land of air.*

St. Kitts

If, as I heard it said, this island is so small
you start running & before you know it
land up in the drink, it would be a preferred death
to what happened at Bloody Point where the river
ran blood & generous plantation owners
donated slaves to build the fort at Brimstone Hill.
Here you have only to reach a certain elevation
before your body temperature drops & your blood
chills & it's true, I felt it even before
our driver told us how, as a boy, he'd picked cotton
for three cents a pound, bags as big as cotton
is light, & he'd pick pebbles to put in the sack
to weigh it down. We drown ourselves in four rum flavours.
You want to make money here you open a church.

Tortola

The mythic Sinbad sailed here, mountains switch-backing
down to God-given bays, *pelicanos* walking
on water before they dive to dine: breakfast juice
fine sugar-cane rum, island-hopping everywhere
six islands, six sailboats, all in a row, nothing
but a Sinbadian fantasy of islands
like roc's eggs, gigantic whales, sea horses, serpents
& black giants till he awoke &, seeing his ship
far out to sea, immediately did what his
tour director had told him to do: took out his
digital & got off a unique one-of-a-kind
shot of his ship, now a speck on the horizon.
But even Sinbad recovered his luggage &
for the price of a small house you too can cruise.

Half Moon Cay

The first fishies we see are make-believe
painted onto the sides of four tanks
like four square bathtubs in the centre of
the Ocean View glass-bottom boat.
You sign the waiver or you don't go.

Columbus. San Salvador. Names
from a past papered over
Yellow-Tailed Snapper and Long-
Nosed Needlefish good for bait.
Coral caves, coral gardens, monster

sting rays 80 feet down, pastel
sea fingers waving. Islands of
limestone coral like chalk. Sand like
icing sugar, snow, powder, flour.
In this Caribbean theme park

we appear to be mere decoration
towel-totting tourists
in paradise, visitors for a day
snorkeling without getting wet.

San Juan II

All night the noise kept us awake. First light
our eyes no bigger than no-see-ums, we make our way
to Mass at the *Catedral,* past houses full of grass
stuffed in shoe boxes hiding gifts, water
for camels at every door, & shouting children
dressed in their Sunday best for the Feast
of Epiphany, the coming of the Three Kings
carved *santos* come to *verissimo* with the baby
Jesus who lies buried beneath a sea of poinsettias
the altar entombed by six Christmas wreaths
& six Christmas trees, collection baskets
like fishing nets, while a black steel serpent
its head a tiny TV, stalks the church twenty feet
above us, recording our every thought. And prayer.

San Juan Rite

for Peter Wilkinson

On the *Catedral* steps crosses outnumber flags.
Now that the daylight fills the sky
the Bishop robed in purple & I in white
pray the Office of Prime. To the sound of
music I hold high a banner of the Saint
and we begin to *walk in the law of the Lord*
down del Cristo to Puerta de San Juan to the sea.

Our processional grows each city block
cross-streets like pews, like rivers to the sea
as people stream in behind us, from Sol, Luna
San Sebastian, San Francisco, fishermen
on their way to work, workers in procession to the fields
each *calle* a pathway, each corner or station
a pausing point, a stanza for prayer or recitation.

While we pass the day on the walkway, wives
& lovers bring us pina coladas, crab cakes and high tea
as we pray through Terce, Sext, and None till Compline
comes & priest & acolyte, workers & fishermen reform
and proceed back up the blue cobblestone streets
a processional like salmon swimming upstream
returning to their homes to spawn further *familia.*

~ 41 ~

Reflective River of Stars & Stone

(a South American Sequence)

Maria Antigua Guatemala

She's 15 — or 40 — with a presence
that calls on 4000 years, a woman
selling red, black and orange bracelets
up and down the dirty cobblestone streets.
Her country's costume is the dress she wears.
I ask her if she wants to come on the bus.
She looks through me and sees the end of her world.
Her face fills with Mayan exhaustion.
This is clearly not the passage she seeks.
She promises to think about it for 52 years.
She tells me she wants our way to go back
to the past; only then will our under-
standing take us into a whole, new world
of things *never seen or dreamed of before.*

Dying of Thirst

for Lisa, with thanks

Like nature's gargoyle erupting over
the Basilica the bougainvillea flows

down the red brick wall like volcanic lava.
In the *Catedral* I am guided to the roof to see the city

spread out before me but the bougainvillea
like male peacocks, everywhere obstructs the view.

One gringo kid called Peter
has been dragged up here to see distant mountains

with the promise he'll soon drink from the magic
fountain in the inner courtyard below.

The pink stone turns the moat to mortal green
as we make our way over the stone bridge

to the fountain's side & the wiped-out whiny kid
wiping out any hope of a meditative moment

breaks loose from his weary parents &
steps off the bridge onto what he believes

to be grass. I really do love kids
but once in a while they get what's coming to them.

The Maya Codex

Mayan scribes sit facing one another.
Their headdresses full of coloured feathers
sometimes fall forward, obscuring their sight
of the hundred tiles that form a perfect
square between them on the earthen floor.
The Tonsured Maize God or super-scribe
takes account of every turn and tile
each one of which in hieroglyphic script
reveals the image of an animal —
anteater, butterfly, cock-of-the-rock
river dolphin, eagle, three-striped poison frog
gecko, heron, iguana, jaguar
to llama, yellow-tailed woolly monkey
owlet, puma, spiny rat, mushroom-tongued
salamander, twist wing through to whale
a grand opening alphabet of words.
Over time the scribes speak but have no way
of writing down what they say or think.
They take turns turning over the wood tiles
play the game for centuries together
the way it should be played. Many moons
pass before they understand they have uncovered
a written language one letter at a time.
To this day the two scribes still play *Scrabble*
while the Tonsured Maize God or super-scribe
continues to add the infinite score.

Nicaragua Soldata

Glory . . . is a flock of buzzards in a field and a great stink.
— Ernesto Cardenal

Brown white-beaked-bellied boobies fish as far
inland as lakes famous for fresh water
sharks. Corinto exports only travel
and flight. The highway, a volcanic ring
burns sesame seeds and sugar-cane fields.
On the bus (Mercedes-Benz) we are at
the mercy of Padre Diego
brooding tour guide & Field Chaplain of the
Sandinistas, who speaks of *a nation*
of poets, & warns that when the Bishop
of Leon sits beside the government
his money-lined vestments change people from
poor Christinas to poor Sandinistas.
No trace of a smile crosses Diego's
dark face when he adds that *some sins are best*
left for the church, others only to God.

Swimming with Turtles

Oblivious to us they feed then rise
to the surface, *turtles all the way down*
floating regally for centuries
without predatory fear, as if by
magic, above seaweed beds and
sargassum weeds, learning how to grow
wise in the warm Gulf stream current.

They still have half a hundred years to swim
each a survivor, one in one thousand
who've made it beyond birds and devil crabs.
Worshipped by the first century Moche
the mythological Turtle Mother
holds the whole world on her speckled back
in the Cays off the Nicaraguan coast.

I stretch far out over the ship's rail to
see my flat open hands turning turtle
to receive these prehistoric creatures
encased in armoured shells, swimming with
delight in their innate serenity
floating free in a bottomless world.
It's green sea *turtles all the way down.*

A Taste of Costa Rica

On a four hour bus tour through the highlands
humidity transforms us to farmers
taking our crop to Puerto Caldera
to sell to long ships that line the harbour.
It feels like we've been walking for a week
for 500 years, our decorated
ox carts filled with coffee beans, our kerchiefs
bleached to ribbons in the stultifying heat.
Out of boredom we spend our final night
in Esparga, in the public square that
serves as a kind of limbo or a front
porch to the church for those who hesitate
to awaken & embrace the faith.
After dark our people pray in the river.
As if in a dream we pass through groves of
mangoes, pineapples, bananas, cashew
trees, oranges, watermelons, cantaloupes
fields of rice and paprika, plantations
of sugar-cane, coffee, chicken farms
the night animals never far away.
Volcanic sulphur turns the soil dust red.
Fallen coconuts grow themselves green.
We imagine if we stay here too long
we'll be rooted forever. In this place
money really grows on trees; no one
goes to the store to buy anything.

Sonnet on the Real Presence in Panama

Carnations and lilies line the sanctuary
near palm trees that welcome wild birds to the *Altar
de Oro.* The humidity waters the bowels.
Twelve giant fans drown out all amplified voices.
We sing several revolutionary hymns.
Farmers and fishermen become the Apostles.
Tourist buses dump more human cargo down the
side aisles where, devoid of imagination, they
take a shot of something they can't see or believe.
We take the Sacrament on our knees. After the
Blessing, the organist plays a marimba beat
accompanied by two bongo players and twin
tambourines, while the Real Presence lives outside
with the poor in their shanty towns of mud and tin.

Guayaquil

High tide as we chug our way four hours up
the Guayas River, jungle granny-apple
green to the chocolate water's edge.
Trader tankers line up like enormous
iguanas waiting to be fed, the whole
river a spawning ground for yellow fever
pirates and revolutionaries.
Layers of culture build one atop the
other: tribal, Indian, Spanish, mestizo, modern.
Shrove Tuesday, the market closed, the streets
empty, churches filled with pick-pockets
praying, plenty of poor people to feed
full of revolutionary ideas.
Well-dressed Pablo smoking a cigar.
Up north, in Quito, where *personalismo*
reigns supreme, Moreno the Great begins
his day by reading *The Imitation*
of Christ to his assembled family.
Up in the Crow's Nest, the storm clouds break to
reveal an Inkan doorway lighting up
the dark sky. Thunder knocks. We pass on through
to a different place. The heavens open.

Somewhere Around Trujillo

I El Brujo

On highways to country roads to irrigation paths
we are driven to the beginning and end of the Earth
fronting the sea, sand dunes like giant ant hills behind
us mountains and mist. Fields of green herbs rise from
fallen revolutionaries, their bodies choking
the irrigation canals our bus inches by.

Images abound on the adobe walls of this sacred city.
Nude prisoners, ropes wrapped about their necks
march in rows to the Sorcerer god, whose body is all
animal, a constellation of catfish, owl
eagle, crab, ray fish, to feed the Mochian people.
The Sorcerer of snakes and skulls begins to smile.

High drifting sands conceal more than dry coastal tombs.
A huge spider carries the obsidian knife.
Campfires turn the earth into a star-studded sky.
The route to the water has a reputation.

II The Citadel of Chan Chan

Their god came in on a sea of balsa rafts
worshipping the moon and stars, and so they could see
to work and play by the light of both night and day.

~ 52 ~

Mud walls 15-feet thick and 60 feet high are
filled with fish that go up and down with the stylised
tides, and happy pelicans out for a walk
hold their tails overhead like umbrellas, birds
brought down to earth with sea shells and sea otters.

Sacred signs on carved stones, frescoes we created.
Perhaps there is something up there we've overlooked
in the dark, invisible space between stars.

III   Huaca de la Luna (Moon Temple)

Are we surprised the nude prisoners have marched
over here, 30 miles to the East? Now they walk
with dancers in tunics, Priests-of-the-Solar-Cult
deer hunters, sea-lion warriors with weapons, big
spiders and soldiers carrying fish, felines with
reptile bodies holding human heads in their paws
a boa constrictor with serpent belt buckled
with a black condor head, and the brown ceramic
Warrior Duck with duck-spoon beak asleep in an
egg-shaped relief of ochre mixed with cactus juice.

Sand covers the ancient symmetrical city.
The unexcavated Huaca del Sol sits
a mound of muddy earth fragile in front of us
for the next El Niño to bring down.

Star pottery. Moonstone permits no one to sit.
If you don't know what to do you look to the sky.

~ 53 ~

Cuzco

for César, sovereign guide

Condor Airlines glides in, 11,000 feet
above the sea. Gasping for breath we fall into
the past, into mountain sickness, dizzy spells
nausea, our chins vanish, foreheads recede , cheekbones
twitch, our skin burns copper, a million years
of evolution takes but an airport minute
in this rarified Andean air. We are
determined to become Inka. Inka — or die.

We gulp down cocoa-leaf tea, swallow coca-
sweet candies until our Quechan guide, a caged
puma, appears anxiously in the lobby of
our five-star inn (the original home of
Francisco Pizarro). César's aquiline nose
twitches as he shoulders the silent solidity of
500 hundred years of history
outside to wait for us in the polished rain.

Across the cobblestones sits Santo Domingo
a massive baroque church built upon what
lies beneath. We pray our own prayers
join the spirits of 4000 Inka priests
the last half-dozen Dominicans.
In the golden courtyard rain blesses our foreheads.
We are in the great Inka Temple of the Sun.
You can see where the Dominicans stole the gold.

César falls to his knees before a single stone
praying we will see the bevelled interlocking blocks
the dark polygonal patterns, no two stones alike.
He is an Inkan poet building a wall
bringing it back to life.
Above us, Jesus & friends eat guinea pig
drink maize beer, while the Lord of the Earthquakes rises
to live forever like a sacrificial lamb.

And César? He lives for nothing less
than to serve the cosmos, restore
the natural order of his stone nation
fingering its cold Inka resistance.

Postcards from Cuzco

Who is the Inka God responsible
for this rain I'd like to know.
Get El Señor on his cell phone immediately.
From a *dark secluded place*
the call rings through to the front desk.
The Inka Rain God has spoken truly.
The lost city is lost to us, our travel plans
buried by landslide, drowned by Noah's flood
with no hope of a rainbow
our world turned upside down.

∾

Like Moses in the Promised Land
we saw it from afar
from the Sacred Valley
but could not enter that humid mountain retreat.
At my age I could not have climbed those sacred peaks.
I am one tired stone.

∾

Yet our time in Ollantaytambo —
a Machu Picchu in silhouette —
pre-Columbian cobblestoned streets now scarred
by tour buses, American hippies
Japanese and German contemporary
conquistadores bent on sacrilegious sacking

the tidy-terraced Temple of the Sun now
an urban nightmare reserved for tourists
crawling with people like an army of red ants
made us feel we no longer needed to see Machu Picchu.
(What poet would deliberately misspell a place name to make it his own?)

∾

Was it all a Utopian dream of llama paths and pyramids?
Knock three times and whisper low.
Say Ernesto's brother Fernando
called it *the place where the revolutionaries hid* .
A kind of Hernando's hideaway?
I am a brick-layer surrounded by Inka stone.

That Moment Falling Through Air

On Sunday afternoon, February the nineteenth, 2012, I crossed the fictional bridge of San Luis Rey, *the finest bridge in all Peru that broke and precipitated five travellers into the gulf below. That moment falling through air.* As if tossed from a wind-stripped hammock.

Was it accident or plan? What had Thornton Wilder been reading? Smoking? I struggle to see the author in his hotel room in Zurich in a trance-like state, hard at work on his final draft of the novel in a five-star Swiss establishment, the Alps outside his window becoming the Andes he'd never seen.

There is no gulf, no narrow torrent *hundreds of feet below,* no rafts, no Inca-rope osier-woven suspension bridge *on the high road between Lima and Cuzco:* it is made of concrete, in the *Centro de Lima,* a few blocks from Santo Domingo and the literary academy. I found no archaeological evidence that *servant girls returned bracelets which they had taken from their mistresses.* But our Inca guide perpetuates the myth.

I cross the conventional, modern bridge. There is no *little mud church on the far side.* I try to imagine the bridge *suspended on the high-road between Lima and Cuzco, a mere ladder of thin slats swung out over the gorge, with handrails of dried vine* and how *horses and coaches and chairs had to go down hundreds of feet below and pass over the narrow torrent on rafts.*

But it is no go. The bridge fell. Like the twin towers. We know what happened to those people. Through anger, pain, grief and doubt, they continue to be — loved. On my only visit to the city I crossed the bridge I intend to cross again.

~ 58 ~

Latin American Poetics

Latin American poets are so poetic

  — not their poems so much as their shape-shifting
name-changing names like Pablo Neruda
Octavio Paz or my favourite, Ernesto Cardenal.

  Think about it. Say the names.
Say their names. Say any two names aloud.
What chance does the name Doug Beardsley have

  against such inventive, ringing, singing
Latin American names? What right have I got even to write
with such a dull, boring, flat, stumbling-block of a name?

Only Aubrey matters and look what happened to him.

South of the Equator

Linnie

The sea is desert
flying fish like
glittering waterwheels
in surrendering circles

& that line across
the camera image
is the celestial
equator made real

& late last night
when I told you you'd achieved
the impossible
& were now more beautiful
than when we met

we stayed that way, way beyond
the shipping lanes, the
globe-trotting yachts
our posture of expectancy
perpendicular to the earth.

Was it light from another
ship perhaps, pinpoints
on the horizon halfway
between the poles?

First Landfall at Nuku Hiva

Black lava ridges, scaly spines of sea
dragon lizards, creepers, coconuts
rotted black, basking
in the sun; what Stevenson called
the silence of expectation
hovers over us. We see whatever
we bring to the cocoa palms
(I write psalms!) breadfruit trees
the pagan gods stoned
like cannibal ghosts after the sun
drops into its circular
tunnel under the sea.
We are all wooden tikis
carved by water & wind
skulls like ostrich eggs
home for the hermit crab
the tiny fruit bat.
We are squeezed small
by sea dragons, tiki idols
& 'god botherers'
as we walk the first island
lost at the beginning of the earth.
Dawn comes *of a sudden* so close
to the equator.

Tahiti

In Papenoo Valley the whispering water
falls three hundred feet over the rocks
stone columns becoming human
figures piled upon figures cascading
in contemplative prayer

The Power of the Marketplace

At the market in Papeete a very towardly
Tahitian in mauve dress
smiles at me (no ordinary smile) plucks
a mango (my favourite fruit) from her stall
rubs it back & forth over her
brown, bare, cinnamon belly then offers
to sell it to me for a thousand francs.

Aboard ship, the Captain grabs
the contraband fruit & dashes it
to the deck. I think of the prohibition
against transporting fruit to & from the vessel.

But that night, in the bar, the Captain speaks of how
I've been tabooed, of how Tahitian women cast
spells by rubbing fruit over their bodies
to seduce men & how
from this time forward, she must always be obeyed.

The Vision After the Sermon

We don't know the necessary
accidents that made Gauguin divide the
hemispheres into two weightless worlds
with the diagonal of a tree —
blacks, yellow-whites & reddish-browns

ultramarine, chrome-yellow, other-
worldly orange & bottled green
imagined from the luminous
reef, purples like coral shells
offering an inner peace.

Where myth meets rite
is no more than a blood-earth seed
a thin arbutus tree
clouded with haloed leaves
a metaphysical mystery.

What lies directly in front of us
we sometimes see, but what we
truly see is what we believe

beyond the tree that pathway of pure vermilion

Moorea

Island suburb of Tahiti, the Lido
      of the Southern Hemisphere
suspended from clouds
      on rays of water light.
Our taxi driver, St Cecilia, says
      the island hasn't changed
since she was born some years ago.
      What writers worth their salt
would dare to work on
      a doorstop-sized novel
in this tiraira air?

      Gauguin mooched on Moorea
three years trying to become
      the Messiah of the New
Art, fishing for snake-lizards
      with red wings, luminous
red bananas, alligator pears
      orange earth, yellow hills
& mauve mountains, striving
      to congregate Polynesian myths
with Christian rites, to paint over
      any trace of human habitation.
A significant wind creates the
      rustling in the mind, the time
of day, the sun held high
      the currents stirred to blue-
in-green aquamarine
      the roar of breakers on brown coral.

There is a singular beauty here
         the one truth a pleasing grace.
We fall to our knees under the palms
         waiting to be blessed or
martyred by a coconut with blue leaves.

Bora Bora

Smokestack mountain worthy of the Princess Tahiti
the best of Melville's *five-and-twenty heaps of cinders*
reptilian rock *magnified into mountains*, what Spanish
whalers called the Encantadas.
On Bora Bora you learn about
culture by going to church.
Here they breast-feed in pews
practice the hula in reflective doors.
Smiling women sit in front, men behind like ancient
warriors, gentle giants fierce only in love.
Whites, drained of blood, sit to one side, the dull
glazed eyes of the prune-lipped English sporting
their Sunday-best disapproving stares.
Three ministers, dressed like naval officers
preach in three languages. Everyone
sings hymns by heart , swaying in iambic
pentameter. From the hula
church they learn how to love
how love leads to a larger life.

Fiji

In my watery island dream, motus-shaped melting
pots guard the port while strong-teethed natives
dressed in uniforms of the Fiji
Police Band wave their instruments like clubs
smack their fulsome lips & rub their belly-mats
chanting 'come for dinner' as we Long Pigs
disembark the *Amsterdam* to begin what
was once upon a time a weekly rite.
Few cruise ships dock at Suva now, a dying
city, bridges caved in, streets littered with empty tins of spam
& corned beef. Snorting snot, Armstrong drools as he
drives us to Orchid Island floating in a mangrove
swamp where Jonathan, the heavy-handed giant
offers us a guided tour of the ancient
temple & its head rock, lingers
for a moment at the row of skull smashers
stone clubs with a five-inch nail that with one
blow would crack a skull straight through the crown
without breaking bone, a perfect prize for some ancestral
spirit or high Mari god.
Hearts & tongues are claimed by chiefs
children received the hands & feet.

I've had enough of this supernatural
'Ripley's Believe It or Not' & cry out
'It's five o'clock, dear, dinner time
it's time to return to the dock.' The pot hisses
long knives & brain forks surround us.
here's no going back, we've been transformed
into gifts for the gods, our sacrifice for their manna
salt water seeping from our eyes. I hear you say, 'Love
I don't like the way they're looking at us'
but it's too late, we'll never wake up.

Samoa, September 29, 2009

When the ocean came ashore Frankie had no time
to decide whether it was a test or a gift from God
wiping out the past. *Dis hotel has a history,* Frankie
tells me, giggling, as if *having history* is a bad thing.
His story begins at 7 a.m. at the Rainmaker
Inn, housekeeping the two rooms overlooking the bay.
Between the third & fourth aftershocks
the flat water, calm beyond belief, begins
began to ripple — then bubble
(*Like jello when you put it in the refrigerator*)
a 10-foot tsunami forcing the whole village
(minus 42 school children) to run up
the mountainside. *The floods
stood up in a heap.* Now Frankie knows
what stirs the flying foxes into flight.

Squire Stevenson Arrives in Apia

'Godbotherer' Clarke thought he'd become
part of a play within a play —
the scene where Lord Hamlet
welcomes the wandering players
to Wittenburg, the ones who'd fallen
on hard times. But this was a two-man, one-
woman entertainment sailing into Samoa.

Fanny in print gown, crescent
earrings, small-shelled wreath
plaited straw hat, scarlet scarf
plaid shawl, white canvas shoes
& across her back like a tattoo
a blue guitar, her son in clown
pyjamas looking like a Scottish trader.

While the Tall One, Teller of Tales
wore shabby white flannels, a tattered
shirt & jaunty yacht cap
which did nothing to conceal
the skeleton of breadsticks & brittle bones
that was all that made up
what was left of the man.

From the Journal of Stevenson's Wife

Each time he goes there, descending
through locked laboratory doors to the
centre of his night creeping, twitching
like a Samoan dog in sandy sleep, images
assault him: crates, papers, bottles, chemicals
powders, books & charts ravaged by white ants

till Fanny, hearing him cry out 'Jen, Jen'
brings him back to this world
(wife dutifully waking disturbed husband)
who sits up in bed waving wildly
screaming 'Pen! Pen!'
at the top of his damaged lungs.

RLS

He would turn in mid-air
to reach for his carved Samoan flute
adorned with the necessary gods
sticking their tongues out at the world
warding off emptiness. Or
he'd donkey-down to Apia
in search of the right word or phrase.

Samoans treated Lewis like a nobleman
entitled to specific language
set apart for him: words we'll never know
for bug, blood, leg, face, hair, belly
eyelids, sleep, dreams, ulcers, cough
sickness, death: not everyday words but
uncommon words from his mysterious world.

Flim Flam Island

for Dale & Marilyn

Far from the fields of morning
       glory once used as camouflage
Sam, our driver
       acts like an island Bogey
as we turn off the side road
       up a goat-trail, fresh grass
weaving between our worn-out tires.
       Two white shells
       mark the path's entrance.
We are promised a cultural village
       fire-walkers so fierce
it's going to cost us eighty dollars
       up front as Sam goes some ways
beyond, turns his taxi round
       while we begin to mark our way up the trail
calling out the fire-walkers
       eager to offer us the most authentic
imaginable, real fire-walkers
       walking on real coals in *real time*.
       We await the promised call
       of the conch, aware only of the silence.
Perhaps the shills are still
       sleeping, resting their burnt soles
having spent a second too long
       on the slow-burning coals, I think
as we see the last
       visible sign of Sam, the

confidence man, disappear over the hill
       and little else
beyond the two white shells but
       bush becoming more bush.
If we had walked that way
       we'd have come
to a burnt-black clearing
       & a brown boy in white underwear
living a life
       of missed opportunities
our long shadows disappearing
       down the road
within sight of our sailing ship.

Terra Australis Incognita

A continent tale of three
  cities: Cairns, Brisbane, Sydney
the triangle feared by all
  convicts and slaves, places birthed
by blackbirding, flogging & the lash
  played out as national sports
like horse-breeding & racing
  children practicing on gum trees
cut down to size, tall-poppied
  in a soul-less silent emptiness of
'wait-a-while' palms
  & bird-nest ferns like baskets
shared by twenty million somewhere
  beyond the southern imagination.
What we feel in this triangle of
  cities counts for something —
each has a social conscience
  fresh, new, civil, wealthy
its horrible history
  nowhere to be seen.

Macho Madness

When my wife asks me to stay
close to the valuables she's left
on the lounge chair on the Lido deck
while she goes to check the wash
the Aussie stranger at the ship's rail
leans behind his lovely *damsel*
with a dulcimer voice & in a confident
whisper says, 'A few too many
instructions, mate' & I begin
to wonder what makes a man
in Gondwana Land. Then I read
of their desert inscape
the terrifying emptiness & haunting
silence at the centre of this place
& how bushrangers who made
drinking a national disease
needed a mate simply to survive.

Pamagirri Dances

In Far North Queensland
    time the boys roll stones
down mountains & beat them

to the bottom where the girls
    drop them down their dresses
  praying for an easy birth

or so the Songman sings
    his arms & legs bound
  with sinews to ward off evil spirits

as he welcomes the new world
    to the Corroboree
  at the Rain Forest Station

in Kuranda where the Pamagirri
    perform their sacred dances
  in the absolute reality of this world

in the magic circle they make
    on stage in front of us
  becoming the thing itself

the kangaroo, koala, dingo, emu
    silent snake &
  the flightless rainforest bird

Arkana (Auckland)

(in memory of Susie Middlemass)

Eastward into the rising wheel of the sun
high above the Land of the Long White Cloud.
We fly like albatross over the Tasman Sea to the looking
glass land of flying animals & flightless birds
foxtails, tomtits, kakapos, kiwis, moas
insects like giant wetas, Norwegian ants
walking things like mongoose, tuatara & red deer
left behind when the Moa-Hunters
were swallowed up by seafarers touching noses
touching God's art with out-thrust tongues, *contortions*
spears and guns speaking 'come ashore and we will
kill you,' warding off evil worlds upon worlds
like layers of strata rock: convicts, traders, settlers, sailors
missionaries & Maoris, North Island fish-
hooked from the Pacific, British Isles of the South Seas
fertile Sussex, green Essex beneath us *a solemn*
stillness holds rolling hills and fields in this City of Sails
where Abos, when seen, are seen as cultural performers
warriors who would offer whitey ammo
water & food to prolong the fight, reduced to ritual
song & dance men going through the motions of a natural
life once filled with meaning, their clay
cup broken now. What we uncover *is a piece of the past*
flying through time at precisely the right angle.

Hula Hymns

If I were called in / To construct a religion / I should make use of water.
— Philip Larkin

First Sighting

One hour out of Hilo
(which way are we going?)
    out of this morning's mist
one more illusionist island
    of cloud and fog —
Cook's men see them
    everywhere they look
set sail toward

    nothing. We've been out
four nights — they sail
    four years two months
twenty-two days with little
    wood & no women.
The absence of both proves fatal.

    Like a monster humpback
breaching, Hawaii looms
    the best of Pele's digging
burrowing to escape
    his sister's wrath
a spent deity raising atolls
    an archipelago —
pieces of eight.

    In the marketplace
Hawaiians envelop us
                tugging at our loose skins
the drawers of our trousers

~ 84 ~

from which we draw treasure
over two centuries &
    nothing's changed —
we consume everything

    whatever we can
buy or steal. We have come from
    a cold country at a time
when provisions are low.
    Better us than them the Captain says
thinking in the old way —
    a way of thinking
we'll have to change
    if we're going to survive.

Melville's Mountains

On the starboard watch as the crew parties below
(every night New Year's Eve) he leans against the bulwarks
gazing upon the shoreline to learn what he can
about the bay never raising his eyes

to the undulating hills, those sloping spurs
like flying buttresses to a higher heaven
(his passage to the green mountains) the place
where natives make a meal out of you.

When Melville jumped ship he became a blue whale
worth a bounty of calico rum rations
midshipman's nuts & tobacco plugs
for the foraging parties at the Pioneer Inn.

By the time they gathered in the run-down courtyard
the great writer was on the move north up Front Street
Baldwin House to Wo Hing Temple (not yet a museum)
Papalani to the Sugar Cane Train that leaves five after the hour.

He caught it and rode that steam engine hard
passed Kanapali Golf Course through the sugar cane fields
now a coffee farm but once upon a time
so thick with cane it ate the air until

out of breath, a free man for the moment, Melville
sat munching coconuts three thousand feet above his
ship unaware of the mysterious presence
of natives as cane-like as the killer reeds.

Messenger

. . . let the sea make a noise, and all that is therein.
— Psalm 96

Humpbacked, stout, knobby, countenance like a kahuna
his bulky body cloaked in basic black & white
conservative with a need to congregate a group.
On the verge of extinction, he is easy prey for
the avaricious, modern mind. Shrouded in mystery
he can only take up his position & let loose
his liturgical song: a heavenly cacophony of
doleful groans, yups, oos, woos, foos, mups & up
an underwater *magnificat* fifty fathoms
deep. The more spirited the song the more
mysterious. All powerful, all glorious, he
cruises the high seas, wintering in Hawaii
avoiding the acoustic fog. Only the male sings.

Sacrificial Presence

You shall destroy their altars, break their sacred pillars,
and cut down their wooden images. — Exodus 34

i

Searching for a perfect port
(dare I say Sandwich?)
Cook conducted his men

on a tour of the Hawaiians
for seven weeks
without touching land

his ships like temples
floating altars
ladders to the sky.

The fair breeze blew
the white foam flew
the endless Pacific

wrinkle-free, while we
reluctant tourists
weather force 8 gale winds

with respect
groundswell from 12 to 18 feet
our ship wallowing in the trough

the California Currents
like long spears
destined for the head, heart & groin

as if the sea
running so high

~ 88 ~

              breaks against the sky
a white whale
                  breaching
          about to devour its prey.

                  ii
While the people were paddling in
                  a talking story
          was told: it was said

Cook blockaded Kealakekua Bay
                  fired cannons at canoes
          sent out armed boats

he breathed fire & smoke
                  from his mouth
          like a sea monster

he sailed without women
                  as if exiled
          from his own land

he carried off idols
                  for firewood
          while quoting Exodus 34

he tore down temple fences
                  to fortify masts
          then invented the Cook Pine

he smuggled women aboard
                  dressed them as
          Elizabethan actors

~ 89 ~

he touched a chief
                woke him
        walked in his shadow

he took so much of everything
                from the people
        it was said that was the way it was.

iii

Cook never knew his role
                he never knew who he was
        supposed to be in the Makahiki feast

the lost god Lono
                the sacred chief self-exiled
        for killing his wife in a divine fit

yet he made all the right moves
                he made a right circuit
        around the island

landing at Kealakekua Bay
                he walked the *Pathway*
        of the Gods

to Hikiau, the main temple
                he *became* Lono
        returned to reinstate

his sacred line
                by deposing Ku
        the mere image of a chief.

iv

On the same day
  his bones were picked clean
  Lieutenant King's log records

things stolen
  stones thrown
  muskets fired

Cook retreating
  to the water's edge
  a lava ledge of slippery shale

the Captain down
  on one knee, pirouetting
  off his Newfoundland-scarred hand

till a blow on the head
  a spike to the neck
  tumble him into the petrified sea

out of his element
  in this cosmic drama
  his bones revered like relics.

v

His-story, mythology
  line against line
  tension of two plays

played out
                    at the same time
            in the same place

a multi-media entertainment
                    one ending
            with Cook discovering the Hawaiians

the other
                    in a legendary battle
            won by Ku

Lono a surrogate god
                    suffering a ritual death
            Cook, profane in space and time

offering *a full, perfect*
                    & sufficient sacrifice
            oblation . . . of himself

while the theatre of the feast
                    returned Hawaiians
            back to the beginning

of their reality
                    where their inner
            & outer worlds were

one.

                    An old Hawaiian proverb says
            chiefs are sharks that walk on land

they leave their ships
            to transcend the past
        shape-shifting to

legends instead
            myth becoming fact
        in a moment without ceasing

to be myth.

Afterword

To give some poems a more Latin American authenticity I occasionally used a Spanish spelling, such as "Catedral" for "Cathedral." In one or two others, I used spellings of the indigenous peoples and their local dialects. For example, when I was in Cuzco, the word "Inca" was spelled "Inka" wherever I walked. However, the Oxford Canadian Dictionary gives only "Inca" as the correct spelling, and this is confirmed by historians John Hemming, Felipe Fernandez-Armesto and the novelist Carlos Fuentes. But what I read and witnessed may have been the most outward ripple of the ongoing clash of cultures and languages more than four centuries after contact. Our Peruvian guide, César, wrote "Inka" and, as well, spelt "Quechuan" as "Quechan." César understood and spoke fluent Spanish, but told everyone he did not know the language. Indeed, the curse of the conquerors' language may well explain the Peruvian spellings in Cuzco and the Sacred Valley. What I experienced in those places was the spirit of the "Inka" sensibility and the "Quechuan" language employed as "a poetics of resistance." I found the assertion of the indigenous "Inka" admirable.